Ric and Ran!

By Raffi Rap

Illustrated by John Nez

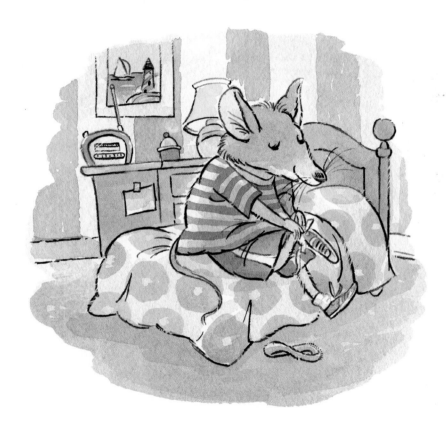

Target Skill Consonant Rr/r/

Scott Foresman
is an imprint of

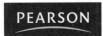

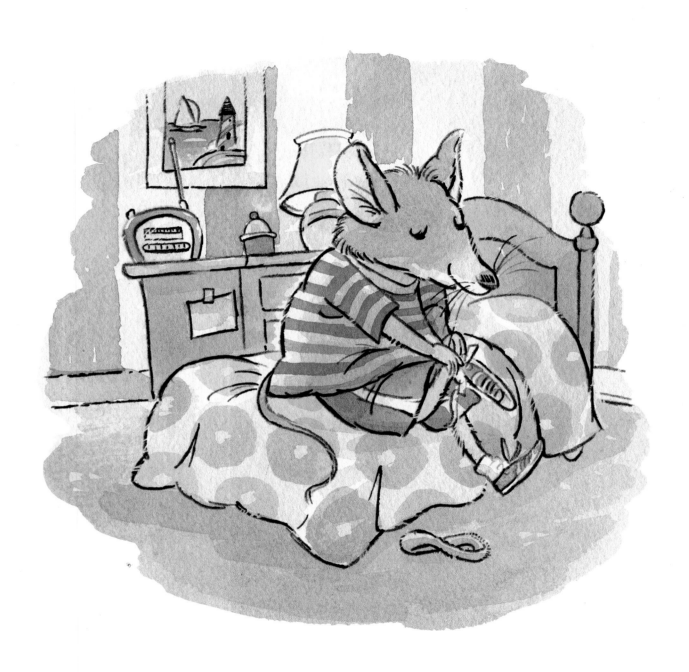

Ric is a rat.

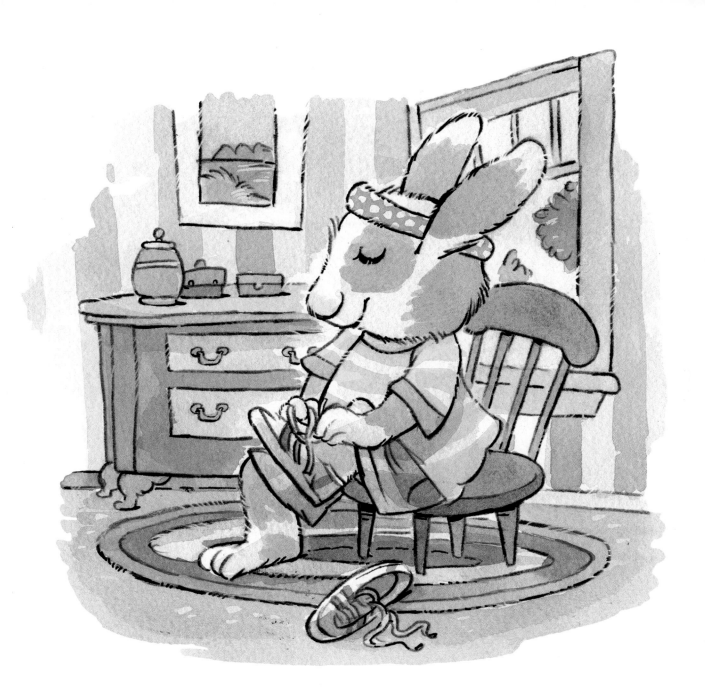

Is Rin a rat?

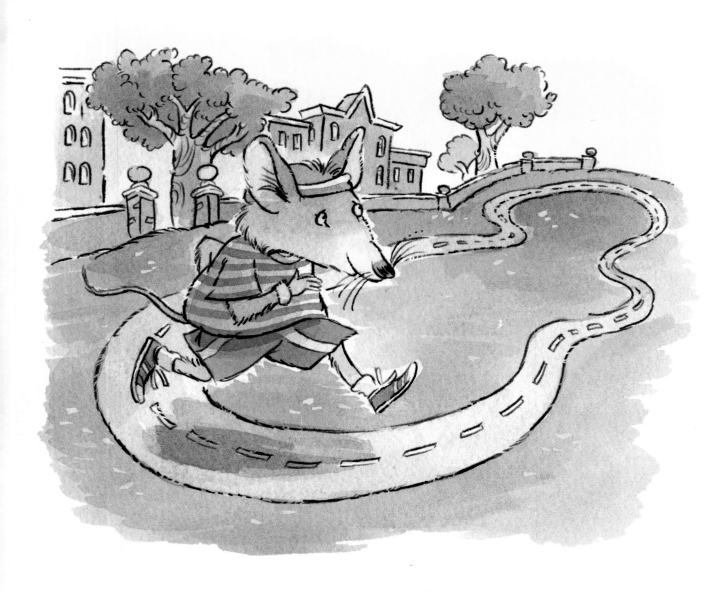

He ran!

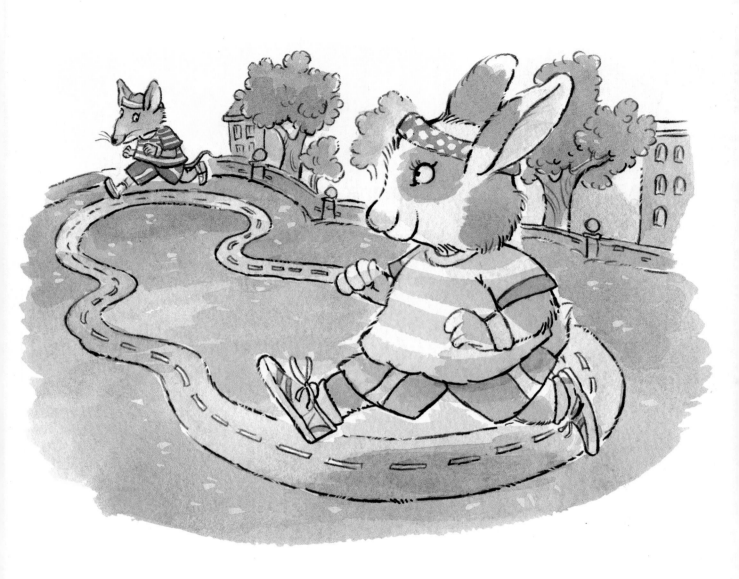

She ran!

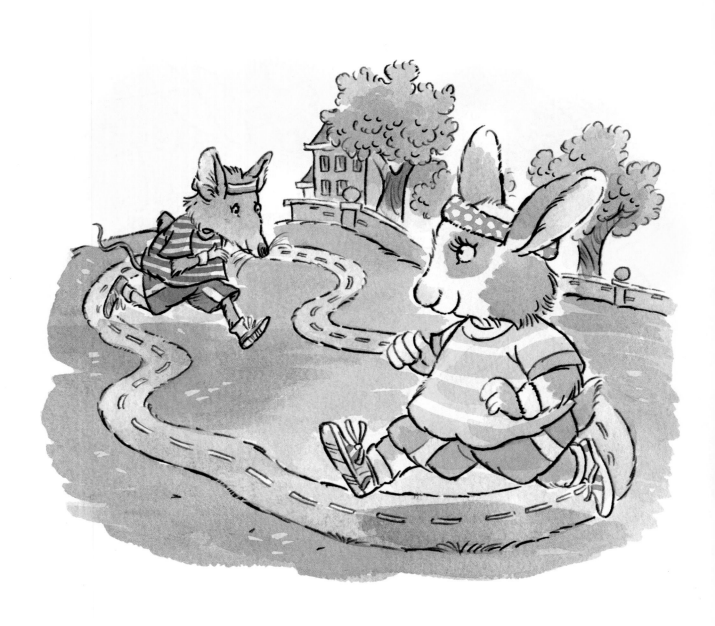

Ric ran and ran.

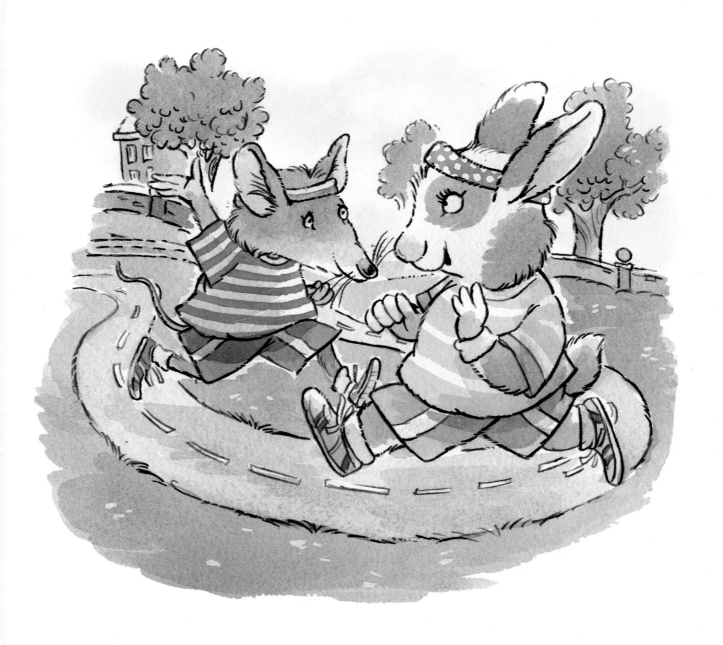

Rin ran and ran.

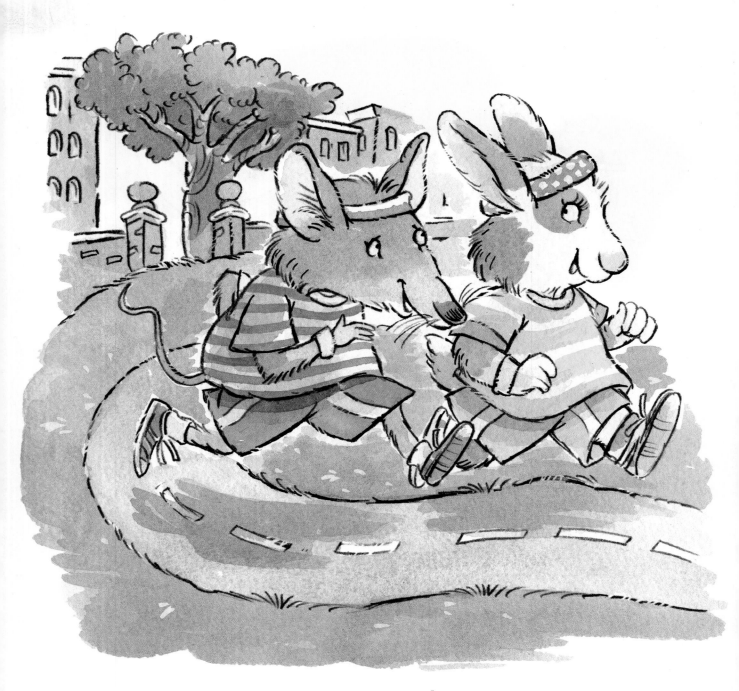

Ric ran with Rin.